Back to Basics™

YEAR 3

NAPLAN*-style READING & WRITING

Do you need to go back to the basics and practise reading and writing for NAPLAN? Let's read together and learn.

Parents and carers are encouraged to read the explanation and practice sections with their child.

Jane Bourke

Illustrated by
Janice Bowles

*This is not an officially endorsed publication of the NAPLAN program and is produced by Pascal Press independently of Australian Governments.

About this book

This book is designed to review the skills required for the Reading and Writing components of the Year 3 NAPLAN test, and to practise NAPLAN*-style reading comprehension questions and writing tasks. The book is divided into 2 main sections: Reading and Writing.

The **Reading** section has 3 levels — beginner, medium and advanced — and contains 11 units, with:

- sample texts covering a variety of text types
- descriptions of the text features
- **We practise** — includes a word bank and colour-coded text features
- **You practise** — comprises 5 comprehension questions with hints.

The **Writing** section contains a 6-page unit for each of the 4 featured text types, comprising of:

We practise

Page 1 descriptions of the features and purpose of the text types

Page 2 annotated analyses of the sample texts, with easy-to-understand colour coding

You practise

Page 3 worksheets to practise the language features

Page 4 planning pages and scaffolding to guide your child through the writing process

Page 5 marking checklists for you and your child to identify any areas that need attention

Page 6 writing exercise pages for your child to create their own texts.

The **16 page, pull-out Reading and Writing test booklet** contains the sample texts to be used for the 9 NAPLAN-style Reading tests and 4 Writing tests to be completed after each unit.

Meet 'BOB' – Back Of the Book

At the end of each unit, BOB reminds your child to go to the back of the book to check their answers.

Contents & Checklist

INTRODUCTION to NAPLAN*

The National Assessment Program for Literacy and Numeracy (NAPLAN) is a Federal Government initiative that requires the assessment of skills in literacy and numeracy across all Australian schools for students in years 3, 5, 7 and 9. It was introduced in 2008 to replace the previous state-based assessment programs.

NAPLAN is held annually in May. All students receive an individualised report on their performance, which can be compared to the average performance of all students in Australia. The report contains a description of each assessment area and identifies the skills being assessed.

Using this book to prepare for the NAPLAN Reading test

The NAPLAN Reading test is based on students reading 6–8 texts and answering up to 8 questions per text. The majority of questions are multiple-choice, where students are required to identify the correct answer to a question by shading the corresponding bubble. Some questions require a short written answer or numbering boxes in a sequence. The Reading units in this book cover the text types and question types used in previous NAPLAN tests.

Using this book to prepare for the NAPLAN Writing test

The NAPLAN Writing test consists of a single page of images and text as a stimulus for writing. The student is asked to write a specific type of text — for example, persuasive or narrative. The Writing units in this book cover the text types that have been used in previous NAPLAN tests, as well as some others that may be used in future tests.

Pull-out Reading and Writing test booklet

The Reading and Writing test booklet contains the 9 reading texts that are used with the 9 NAPLAN-style reading tests in the front section of the book. These are to be attempted on completion of the Reading units. There are 3 tests for each level: beginner, medium and advanced. The booklet also contains 4 NAPLAN-style Writing tests with images and text as a stimulus, and lines to write on. These should be done once the Writing units in the back section of the book have been successfully completed.

It is recommended that your child be timed for each test. This will give your child a good idea of what to expect when they sit for their actual NAPLAN tests.

*This is not an officially endorsed publication of the NAPLAN program and is produced by Pascal Press independently of Australian Governments.

TIPS for TAKING NAPLAN* TESTS

✳ Start by reading the first text in the Reading booklet.
✳ Look at the questions on your test that match the text you have read.
✳ Remember to go back to the text to confirm your answers.
✳ Once you have answered all the questions for the first text, move on to the next one.
✳ Work steadily through the questions, without rushing or dawdling. Don't be put off by an answer that seems too obvious or too simple.
✳ Start at Question 1 and work through the questions in order. If you jump around too much, you risk accidentally missing a question.
✳ Skip any questions that you can't do, rather than spending a long time on them. You might run out of time to do the easier questions!
✳ After you have worked through all the questions, return to any that you skipped earlier and have another go at answering them.

TIMING

You will have 45 minutes to do the NAPLAN Reading test paper, which will have 6–8 questions for each text in the Reading booklet. This means you will have about 7 minutes to read each of the texts and answer the questions about it.

Answering multiple-choice questions

✳ First, try to answer the question without looking at the choices. Once you think you know the correct answer, read through the choices.
✳ Fill in the answer bubble properly

like this ✓

NOT like this  ✗

Exam equipment

✳ Make sure you have at least TWO sharp HB or 2B pencils — in case one breaks.
✳ Make sure you have an eraser — in case you mark the wrong bubble by mistake.

Reading time

✳ Read all the instructions carefully.
✳ Read each question TWICE so you understand exactly what is being asked.

WRITING TEST

The NAPLAN Writing test is held on a different day to the Reading test and runs for 40 minutes. There are no multiple-choice or short answer questions. Instead, you are provided with a single page of images and text as a stimulus, and lined pages to write on.

You will be asked to write a specific type of text similar to the ones in this book. You should spend the first 5 minutes planning your text and 30 minutes writing. This will give you 5 minutes to read over your text to edit and check it at the end.

*This is not an officially endorsed publication of the NAPLAN program and is produced by Pascal Press independently of Australian Governments.

BEGINNER LEVEL

NARRATIVE TEXT: TRADITIONAL FABLE

A narrative is a story that is usually made up. The main purpose of a narrative is to entertain or amuse the reader.
A fable is a short story that usually has animals as characters. It always ends with a moral. A moral tells us the correct way to behave. The title of a fable never hints as to what the moral is.

The ant and the grasshopper

A merry grasshopper was having a great summer's day of dancing, singing and playing his violin. He saw a small, weary ant passing by, working very hard to store enough food for the winter.

"Come and sing with me instead of working so hard all the time," said the grasshopper. "We can have fun."

"I must store food for the winter, when there is none," said the tired ant, "and you should do the same so you have food to eat."

"Winter is a long time away," laughed the grasshopper. But the hard-working ant wouldn't listen and got on with his work.

When the winter came, the starving grasshopper went to the ant's house, begging for something to eat.

"Aha! If you had listened to my advice in the summer, you would not be hungry now," said the ant, full from his evening meal. "You will have to go to bed with no dinner!"

And with that, he closed the door on the poor, hungry grasshopper.

The **moral** of this fable is: *Always prepare for times of need.*

WORD BANK

merry	happy and cheerful
violin	a stringed instrument played with a bow
starving	very hungry
begging	to ask strongly for a favour or for help
advice	an opinion from someone to help you decide what to do

We practise

The adjectives in this story help to describe the characters: *merry, small, weary, tired, hard-working, starving, poor, hungry*

Weary and *tired* are also **synonyms** as they have a similar meaning.

Read The ant and the grasshopper and answer the questions.

Shade ONE bubble in questions 1 to 4.

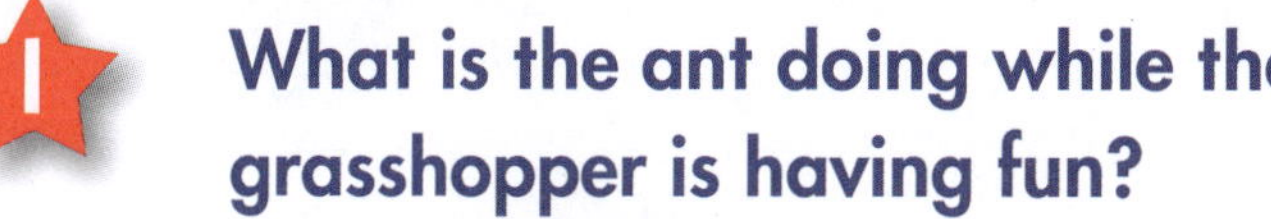

1 What is the ant doing while the grasshopper is having fun?

- ○ gathering food
- ○ sleeping
- ○ eating
- ○ playing the guitar

Read where the grasshopper is having fun and check what the ant is doing at the same time.

2 Why is the ant working hard while the grasshopper is having fun?

- ○ The ant hates having fun.
- ○ The ant is collecting food for winter.
- ○ The ant can't play a violin.
- ○ The grasshopper is rich.

Find the reason the ant gives for not being able to stop and have fun.

3 Why is the ant working hard in summer?

- ○ He doesn't like playing in summer.
- ○ He needs to store food for winter.
- ○ He is bored.
- ○ In winter he likes to go skiing.

4 Why doesn't the ant give any food to the grasshopper?

- ○ The ant doesn't have any food left.
- ○ The grasshopper doesn't like food.
- ○ The ant wants to teach the grasshopper a lesson.
- ○ The ant is busy playing the violin.

Why does the ant shut the door on the grasshopper without giving him the food? The answer is not written in the text.

5 Order these events as they happen in the story. Write 1 to 4 in the boxes.

- ☐ The ant sends the grasshopper away with no food.
- ☐ The grasshopper plays the violin and sings and dances.
- ☐ The grasshopper asks the ant to sing and dance with him.
- ☐ The grasshopper becomes very hungry.

Sometimes the words in the answers are different to those in the story, but they will have the same meaning.

INFORMATION TEXT:

REPORT

The main purpose of an information text is to give information on a topic.
A report usually focuses on one subject or topic — in this case, beetles.
Each paragraph provides different details about the topic. Images and illustrations can provide a lot of information to the reader.

Beautiful beetles

There are many kinds of beetles. They are found everywhere on our planet except in the oceans. Beetles are found in rainforests, scrub, deserts, wetlands and in your backyard. They are able to live in freezing cold areas, yet also in hot springs. They can be happy in freshwater lakes, as well as in dirty and smelly sewers.

Beetles come in many shapes, colours and sizes. Some, such as click beetles and fireflies, are long and thin. Others, like ladybeetles, are round. Most beetles are coloured brown, black or dark red, but some are bright, shiny and even rainbow-coloured.

Like all insects, beetles have three insect body parts: the head, thorax and abdomen. They also have antennae, three pairs of legs and a tough exoskeleton, which is an outside skeleton. Because of the exoskeleton and hard wing covers, beetles are sometimes called the 'armoured tanks' of the insect world.

WORD BANK

scrub the Australian bush where low trees and shrubs grow

wetlands an area where the soil is often wet or always underwater

sewers underground pipes that take away waste water

We practise

Lots of nouns and adjectives are used in information texts.

Nouns: *beetles, rainforests, deserts, ladybeetles, head, exoskeleton*

Adjectives: *dirty, smelly, bright, shiny, hard, armoured*

Read **Beautiful beetles** and answer the questions.
Shade ONE bubble in each question.

1 Which one of these could also be the title of this text?

- ○ The life cycle of a beetle
- ○ All about insects
- ○ The ladybeetle
- ○ Features of beetles

The title states what the report is about.

2 Beetles are not found in

- ○ deserts.
- ○ rainforests.
- ○ oceans.
- ○ mountains.

3 What do the images in this text show?

- ○ All beetles are orange with pink spots.
- ○ Beetles come in different shapes and sizes.
- ○ All beetles have 8 legs.
- ○ Beetles are usually coloured green.

Look at the pictures and rule out the answers that don't work.

4 What three body parts do all insects have?

- ○ horn, hoof, tail
- ○ head, thorax, abdomen
- ○ wings, exoskeleton, bellybutton
- ○ antennae, nose, eyelashes

5 Why are beetles called the 'armoured tanks' of the insect world?

- ○ They like to go to battle.
- ○ They are made of armour.
- ○ Their exoskeleton protects them from harm.
- ○ They run on petrol.

What body feature makes beetles similar to mini armoured tanks?

NARRATIVE TEXT: POEM

The author is trying to give an image of autumn in this poem by using figurative language. Figurative language tells us what autumn sounds, feels and looks like by comparing it to things. The poem shows how the author feels about autumn.

Autumn days

The leaves are a carpet of red, orange and brown,
like crinkled lolly wrappers flying around.
Children play in the leaves piled high,
throwing them towards the autumn sky.
The air is crisp, as cool as ice-cream,
the wind whistles and whispers with ease.
Hidden sun shines low like a lamp in the dark,
a misty fog is a blanket for the trees.

We practise

Figurative language compares things using similes, metaphors and onomatopoeia.

A simile compares two things using 'like' or 'as'.

like crinkled lolly wrappers

as cool as ice-cream

A metaphor compares by saying one thing IS the other.

a misty fog is a blanket

Onomatopoeia is when words sound like the thing they are describing.

the wind whistles and whispers

Read **Autumn days** and answer the questions.
Shade ONE bubble in each question.

What is this poem about?

- ⬭ winter leaves
- ⬭ weather
- ⬭ an autumn scene
- ⬭ children

Which answer best sums up the whole poem?

What is meant by 'the leaves are a carpet'?

- ⬭ The leaves are made of wool.
- ⬭ The leaves cover the ground like a carpet.
- ⬭ The leaves are still on the trees.
- ⬭ The leaves need a vacuum cleaner.

This is a METAPHOR. How are the leaves a bit like a carpet?

Which one of these things is 'like crinkled lolly wrappers flying around'?

- ⬭ children
- ⬭ misty fog
- ⬭ autumn leaves
- ⬭ ice-creams

This is a SIMILE. How would crinkled lolly wrappers fly in the wind?

Why is the sun hidden?

- ⬭ It is playing hide-and-seek.
- ⬭ It is behind clouds and fog.
- ⬭ The sun is very shy.
- ⬭ It is night-time.

The answer is not written in the poem. What sort of day is the author describing? Is it likely to be sunny?

Write two adjectives from this poem.

You have finished the beginner reading level. Now try the reading tests on pages 28–30. Good luck!

MEDIUM LEVEL

PERSUASIVE TEXT: BOOK REVIEW

A persuasive book review gives a clear statement in the first paragraph on what the reviewer thinks of the book. The writer tries to convince the reader to agree with their opinion by giving at least three reasons or examples to back up their opinion. The reviewer explains why they did or did not like the book by describing details such as the plot, the characters, the title and so on.

Persuasive words are used to make a point:
This is definitely the worst book I've ever read.
Sometimes reviews use metaphors or similes:
I would rather watch paint dry than have to read this book.

Book review by Jarrad

On the weekend I read a totally amazing book called *The Adventures of Siegfried and Hannah*. It was such a cool book because it was full of magical journeys to many mysterious lands. You never knew where the characters were going to end up next.

The main characters are a boy called Siegfried (sounds like Sig-freed) and his little sister, Hannah. They are always ready for a mysterious adventure every time they step out their door. The book contains twelve separate stories.

I won't spoil it for you, but what I loved the most was that the main characters were just like real kids. They were the sort of kids that I'd want to be friends with.

I would really recommend that you read this book, especially if you like fairies, dragons, magic, goblins, adventures and surprises. It is the best book I have read all year. There was nothing I did not like about this book, except it should have been longer!

We practise

Use emotive language:
totally amazing, such a cool book, what I loved the most, really recommend, the best book I have read

Use modal verbs:
I *would really* recommend
It *should* have been longer

WORD BANK

mysterious	when something is puzzling and cannot be explained
adventure	an exciting experience
recommend	to encourage something because it is good or useful

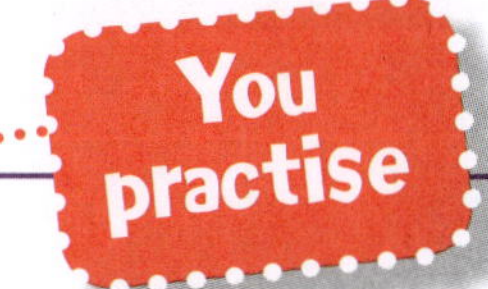

Read the **Book review by Jarrad** and answer the questions. Shade ONE bubble in each question.

1 What sort of book has Jarrad reviewed?

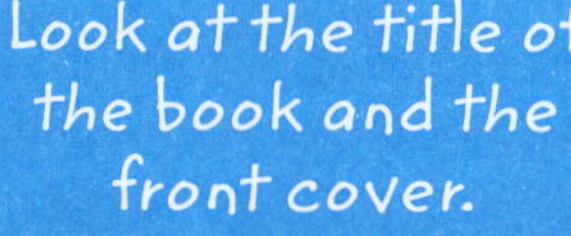

- comic
- historical novel
- reference
- adventure

2 What is Jarrad's opinion of this book?

Does Jarrad use positive or negative words?

- He didn't mind it.
- He really enjoyed it.
- He didn't like the book.
- He thought it was too long.

3 What did Jarrad like the most about this book?

- the number of stories
- the two main characters
- the dragons
- the title of the book

4 Who do you think the audience is for this book review?

Does Jarrad sound like he is using words for children or grown-ups?

- the kids in Jarrad's class
- the teacher
- adults
- people who haven't read the book

5 What does the cover of the book tell you?

- It's a non-fiction book.
- There are elephants in the story.
- The main characters are a boy and a girl.
- It is a book about witches.

BOB time!

INFORMATION TEXT: PROCEDURE

A procedure tells us how to do something.
Recipes, instructions, directions and plans are all types of procedures.

They usually have steps that need to be followed in order. They also include a list of things you will need before you start. In a recipe they are called the ingredients.

Lazy lamingtons

There are 8 steps to this recipe. If they aren't done in order, the recipe may not work.

Lamingtons are an Aussie classic.
This recipe is very easy, as we are using sponge cake that is already made.
These lamingtons are simply delicious and they will be eaten quickly!

Ingredients:

* 1 plain, unfilled, 18 cm rectangular double sponge cake
* 2 cups desiccated coconut

Icing:

* 3 ½ cups icing sugar
* ¼ cup cocoa powder
* 1 tablespoon butter, softened
* ½ cup boiling water

Here's what to do:

1. Sift icing sugar and cocoa into a bowl.
2. Add butter and boiling water.
3. Stir until smooth with no lumps.
4. Cut the sponge cake into 16 square pieces. (One layer = 8 pieces)
5. Place coconut in a dish. Using a fork, dip one piece of cake in icing. Give it a little shake and then roll it in the coconut.
6. Place on a wire rack over a baking tray to catch any drips.
7. Repeat with other pieces.
8. Let them sit for two hours or until set. Enjoy!

WORD BANK

desiccated when something is completely dried out
boiling when a liquid is so hot that it bubbles and steams
sift to put something through a sieve to make it smooth or fine
wire rack a metal structure for holding things

We practise

Lots of verbs (actions and commands) are used in a procedure: *sift, add, stir, cut, dip, roll, place*

**Read *Lazy lamingtons* and answer the questions.
Shade ONE bubble in each question.**

1 How many different ingredients are needed to make these lamingtons?

- ○ 4
- ○ 5
- ○ 6
- ○ 7

Include the sponge cake as one of the ingredients.

2 You have all the ingredients ready to go. What is the first thing you need to do?

- ○ Melt the butter.
- ○ Cut the cake in two.
- ○ Sift icing sugar and cocoa together.
- ○ Stir the icing.

The first thing you need to do is usually the first step of the process.

3 Why does it say to let the lamingtons sit for two hours?

- ○ They like to watch TV before they get eaten.
- ○ It allows the icing time to set.
- ○ It gives you time to clean up the kitchen.
- ○ The lamingtons are made of jelly.

The lamingtons have been put on a rack to catch drips. Why might they need to sit for a while?

4 What does the picture tell you?

- ○ It shows the ingredients that are needed.
- ○ It shows how the lamingtons should look when finished.
- ○ It shows how to mix the icing together.
- ○ It shows how to roll the lamingtons in coconut.

5 Why is this recipe called *Lazy lamingtons*?

- ○ These lamingtons are only for lazy people.
- ○ The lamingtons just like to sit.
- ○ The sponge cake part is already made.
- ○ When you eat these lamingtons, you will feel lazy.

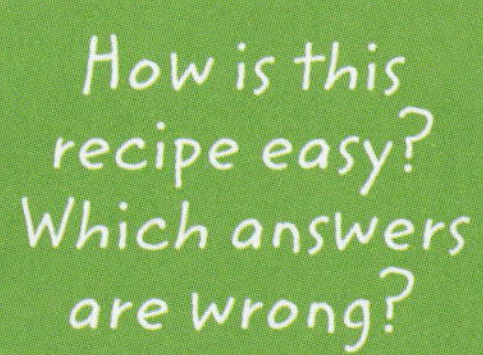

MEDIUM LEVEL

INFORMATION TEXT: EXPLANATION

An explanation tells how or why something happens.
It is used for things like scientific or natural events. An explanation is a little like a procedure as it usually puts the information in steps or stages. Diagrams and pictures are very helpful in explanations to help explain the concept.

How a snowflake is formed

A snowflake begins its life as a tiny ice crystal. This crystal forms when a freezing cold droplet of water vapour freezes onto a microscopic particle in the sky, such as a speck of dust or pollen.

As the tiny crystal falls to the ground, other crystals freeze onto it, building new crystals that then form the six sides (or arms) of the snowflake. The size of the snowflake depends on how many crystals freeze up together.

In most cases, snow crystals form in clouds with below-freezing temperatures. The basic shape of the snowflake depends on the temperature at which the first crystal forms. The flat, plate-like snowflakes are formed in much colder temperatures than the long, needle-like snowflakes. A change in the temperature can change the way a snowflake develops, which is probably why no two snowflakes are exactly the same.

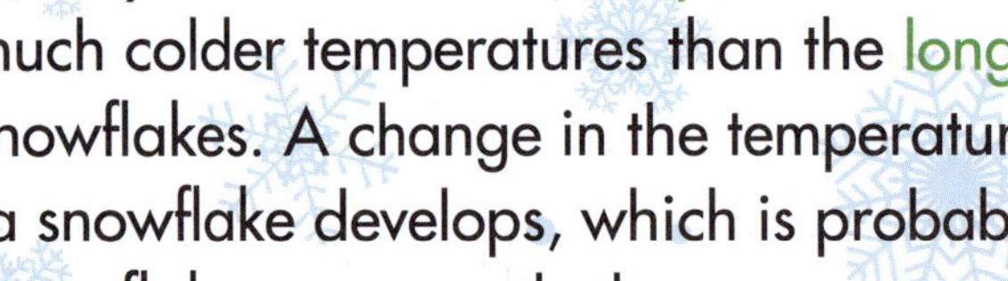

We practise

Use descriptive language (adjectives) to help explain things:
flat, plate-like snowflakes
long, needle-like snowflakes

Explanations are usually written in the present. The action words (verbs) are talking about something as it happens:
'A snowflake *begins* … *forms* … *freezes* …'

WORD BANK

vapour	a gas-like substance
microscopic	something extremely tiny
particle	a very small piece of something
develop	when something changes over time

Read **How a snowflake is formed** and answer the questions.

Shade ONE bubble in in questions 1 to 3.

1 What is it that makes the snowflake turn out a certain shape?

- ○ the number of clouds in the sky
- ○ the number of sides it has
- ○ the amount of water vapour
- ○ the temperature at which the crystal forms

2 What do the images show?

- ○ They show that all snowflakes are exactly the same.
- ○ They show how snowflakes are formed from dust.
- ○ Snowflakes all have six arms.
- ○ Water vapour droplets make snow.

Look at the images and decide which of the choices is true.

3 Which one of these is likely to be the reason why all snowflakes are different?

- ○ temperature
- ○ clouds
- ○ ice
- ○ water vapour

The wording in the text may be a little different to the answer choice.

4 Put these steps in order as they appear in the text. Write 1 to 4 in the boxes.

- ☐ A plate-like snowflake is now formed.
- ☐ Other crystals freeze on as the dust falls.
- ☐ The six arms or sides are formed.
- ☐ The snowflake starts from an ice crystal on dust.

The choices may be worded differently to the text, but the meaning is the same.

5 Which type of snowflake is more likely to form in the coldest temperatures?

____

Read the text where it mentions the types of snowflakes.

BOB time!

UNIT 7

MEDIUM LEVEL

INFORMATION TEXT:

RECOUNT

A recount retells an event in the order it happened. Some recounts are fictional, but some are based on an actual event or series of events. Recounts are often used when retelling historical events. Sometimes they can include personal opinions and emotions as well as facts. It can be told by a narrator or someone who was at the event. In this recount, the narrator was part of the event because pronouns like *we*, *us* and *I* have been used.

Picnic in the forest

It was a cold, wintery morning, but we all rugged up and piled into Uncle Tom's mini-van to head for our forest picnic.

There were seven of us kids and three adults, and what a racket we made!

Everybody was excited about the picnic as we had been planning it for weeks.

We arrived at the forest at 11am and parked the van. First, Uncle Scotty unpacked our gear from the back and we were all given stuff to carry. We had only walked a few steps before Carla dropped her bag. Boiled eggs and lettuce went everywhere. We managed to rescue a few of the eggs, but some of them became food for the lizards!

Finally, we got to the picnic spot, which overlooked a beautiful lake. My mum had made up two big trays of salami and jelly sandwiches and handed them around – YUM.

After lunch, Robbie and I went down to the lake to look for tadpoles. A couple of the older girls even went swimming, but it was too cold for me. We packed everything up and made sure not to leave behind any rubbish.

The walk back to the van was heaps of fun until Marco decided that eating eight sandwiches hadn't been very clever. Up came his lunch all over the place and we had to duck for cover! Even so, we had one of the best days ever.

WORD BANK

rugged up	make yourself warm by wearing thick clothing
racket	a lot of noise and excitement
overlook	look from a higher position
duck	lower your head or body to avoid being hit by something

We practise

Lots of connecting words are used to show the time or order:

first, finally, after lunch

Read **Picnic in the forest** and answer the questions.

Shade ONE bubble in questions 1 to 4.

1 Why was everyone excited about the picnic?

- ⬭ They had never been on a picnic before.
- ⬭ Mum had made salami and jelly sandwiches.
- ⬭ It was near a lake.
- ⬭ They'd been planning it for weeks.

2 What is meant by 'what a racket we made'?

- ⬭ The group made a tennis racket on the way there.
- ⬭ The group were fighting.
- ⬭ The group were very noisy.
- ⬭ The group left a lot of rubbish everywhere.

This group was excited about the picnic. Think of some synonyms for 'racket'.

3 What happened straight after Uncle Scotty unpacked the van?

- ⬭ Carla dropped some boiled eggs.
- ⬭ Robbie looked for tadpoles.
- ⬭ Mum handed around the sandwiches.
- ⬭ Marco was sick.

Look for the answer choices in the text and see what order they happened.

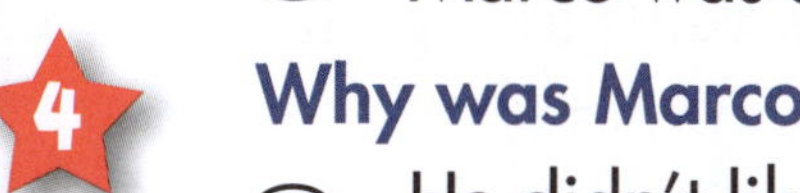

4 Why was Marco sick?

- ⬭ He didn't like salami.
- ⬭ He had eaten too many sandwiches.
- ⬭ He was homesick.
- ⬭ The boiled eggs were off.

What is the most likely explanation for Marco being sick?

5 Order the sentences as they happened in the recount. Write 1 to 4 in the boxes.

- ☐ We handed around two trays of sandwiches.
- ☐ We parked the van.
- ☐ We cleaned up the rubbish.
- ☐ We looked for tadpoles.

The wording in the text may be different to the answer choices.

You have finished the medium reading level. Now try the reading tests on pages 31–33. Good luck!

BOB time!

NARRATIVE TEXT:
TRADITIONAL STORY

Traditional narratives are passed down through the generations by storytelling. All cultures have their own myths and legends. The stories are special to the people who tell them and listen to them, but they are not necessarily true.

A traditional narrative tells a story with a problem and tries to explain how something came to be. In this traditional Aboriginal story, Tiddalik the frog swallowed a lot of water and then created a flood.

The Aboriginal people believe that the stone formation at Wollombi in New South Wales is Tiddalik the frog.

Tiddalik the frog

Indigenous Australian Dreaming Legend: *This is one of the most widely told stories of the Dreaming and has many versions. The story has its origins with the Gunai people of South Gippsland, Victoria.*

A long time ago in the Dreaming, there was a giant frog called Tiddalik. One day he became very thirsty so he decided to drink all the water in the stream. He did not care about the other creatures that needed the water. Soon his stomach was so full that he was ready to burst and he could hardly move.

This made the other animals very upset as there was no water in the stream for them to drink.

After a while, the animals came up with a plan to make Tiddalik laugh so that the water would spill out. One by one the animals tried hard to make Tiddalik laugh with their funny stories and actions, but nothing happened.

The kookaburra told his funniest stories and even laughed at them himself, but Tiddalik didn't laugh. The kangaroo jumped over the emu, but still Tiddalik didn't laugh. The blanket lizard puffed himself up and stuck out his tummy, but none of this made Tiddalik laugh. The animals were starting to get very worried.

Finally, Nabunum the eel tied himself in all sorts of knots and Tiddalik burst out laughing. All of the water came out of his mouth like a huge flood and filled up the streambed, making the animals very happy again. Tiddalik was then punished for being so greedy and was turned into stone.

WORD BANK

stream a small, narrow river

creature a name for any type of animal

burst when something cracks or breaks open suddenly

We practise

Use past tense verbs:
became, was, tried, happened, filled

Use action verbs:
jumped, puffed, tied

You practise

Read *Tiddalik the frog* and answer the questions.

Shade ONE bubble in each question.

1 Why did Tiddalik drink all of the water in the stream?

- ○ He wanted to annoy the other animals.
- ○ He was very thirsty.
- ○ He was very hungry.
- ○ There were many other streams for the animals to drink from.

2 How did the animals feel about Tiddalik drinking all of the water?

- ○ They were cross.
- ○ They didn't care.
- ○ They were happy.
- ○ They thought it was funny.

The words might be different in the text but they will have a similar meaning.

3 Which animal made Tiddalik laugh?

- ○ the kookaburra
- ○ the eel
- ○ the blanket lizard
- ○ the kangaroo

Cross out what did NOT make Tiddalik laugh and you'll be left with the answer.

4 Why were the animals worried when Tiddalik wouldn't laugh?

- ○ They realised that their stories and actions weren't that funny.
- ○ They thought that they would never get their water back.
- ○ They thought Tiddalik was very sad.
- ○ They thought Tiddalik was sick.

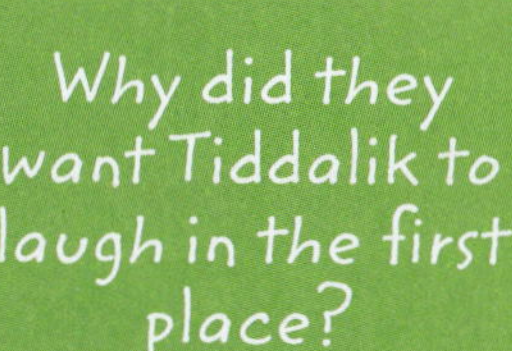

5 Which one of these statements did NOT happen in the story?

- ○ The animals thought of a plan to make Tiddalik laugh.
- ○ The kookaburra jumped over the emu.
- ○ Tiddalik let all the water back into the streambed.
- ○ The eel tied himself in knots.

Read the answer choices carefully. There could be some words there to try and trick you!

BOB time!

ADVANCED LEVEL

PERSUASIVE TEXT: EXPOSITION

A persuasive exposition — also known as an argument — is written to present a point of view for a topic or against a topic.
The main aim is to convince the reader to agree by giving reasons, examples and statistics to support the ideas.

Recycle your rubbish!

Recycling is what happens when we turn our rubbish back into raw materials so that it can be made into new items. However, some people are not bothering to do this and it's not fair to the people that make an effort!

Recycling is very helpful for EVERYONE because it helps our planet. It saves money on making completely new things and therefore we are not using up all of the Earth's natural resources. People who don't recycle are just lazy and don't care about our environment. We need to save the planet for our kids and grandkids to enjoy.

We can also help the environment by reducing the amount of rubbish we make by re-using things like shopping bags and buying refills for products like hand soap. It is a waste to throw out the container when it can be used again.

There are many groups that are set up by very caring people that help us to learn how to recycle. So there are NO excuses for not recycling.

WORD BANK

raw materials	material in its natural state, before it is made into something else, e.g. wool, wood
natural resources	things that occur naturally on the Earth, e.g. sun, wind, water
reduce	to make something less
refills	the material replacing a used-up product
excuse	a reason for not doing

We practise

Use language that is authoritative:
there are NO excuses

Use language that is emotive:
it's not fair
people who don't recycle are just lazy and don't care

Link ideas with connecting words:
however, because, therefore, so

You practise

Read *Recycle your rubbish!* and answer the questions.

Shade ONE bubble in questions 1 to 4.

1 Why does the author think recycling is important?

- ○ It is easy to do.
- ○ It helps our planet.
- ○ It stops you from being lazy.
- ○ It's fun.

What is the main point the author makes?

2 Who is the author writing this text for?

- ○ people who already recycle
- ○ people who are not recycling
- ○ his kids and grandkids
- ○ a recycling group

Who is the author trying to convince?

3 Which statement below sums up this text?

- ○ All lazy people are ruining our environment.
- ○ There are no excuses for not recycling.
- ○ Recycling can save money.
- ○ Recycling is hard work.

4 Which one of these is NOT given as a reason for recycling?

- ○ Recycling saves the Earth's resources.
- ○ Recycling doesn't take up much time.
- ○ Recycling is good for the environment.
- ○ Recycling saves money.

Find the reasons that ARE given and you'll be left with the answer.

5 What is one of the recycling suggestions in this text?

What can we recycle?

____

____

BOB time!

INFORMATION TEXT: EXPLANATION

An explanation gives us information about a specific subject. It includes facts that are put in a logical order. Technical words are used so the writing is more formal and serious.

How honey is made

Bees are amazing insects. They are so busy yet they only live for about 40 days! Bees live in hives and this is where all the action happens.

Inside the hive, the worker honeybees make lots of tiny cells using the wax that comes from their bodies.

The cells always have a hexagonal shape and are used to store honey, pollen and tiny bee eggs called larvae.

The honeybee has a tongue shaped like a tube. This makes it very easy to suck up the nectar from a flower.

The nectar is mostly made up of water and some sugars. The sugars are important in the honey-making process. A bee will visit between 100–1500 flowers before its honey sac is full. The honey sac is like another stomach.

Once the bee arrives back at the hive, the worker bees suck the nectar out of the bee's honey sac. The bees then chew on the nectar to break it down to simple sugars. They then spread the nectar through the cells and use their wings like a fan to cause the water to evaporate. This turns the nectar into a thick, sweet syrup. Once the honey is ready, the bees close the cell of the honeycomb with more of their wax to store it away.

WORD BANK

cell	a small area or compartment
hexagonal	something shaped with 6 straight sides
larvae	the young of any insect that changes the form of its body before it becomes an adult
tube	a narrow, hollow pipe
sac	a structure like a bag
evaporate	when liquid turns to vapour

We practise

Use technical words: *cells, hexagonal, larvae, tube, sac, evaporate.*

Technical words can be included in a glossary or word bank.

Read **How honey is made** and answer the questions.

Shade ONE bubble in questions 1 to 3.

1 What is this text mainly explaining?

- ○ how bees make honey
- ○ where nectar comes from
- ○ where pollen comes from
- ○ how a hive works

What is the author mainly writing about?

2 The honey sac

- ○ is never full.
- ○ needs nectar from 50 flowers to fill up.
- ○ can only be used once.
- ○ is where the bee stores the nectar.

Find in the text where 'sac' is mentioned and read that part carefully.

3 How does the nectar become thick?

- ○ Wax is added to it.
- ○ The water in it evaporates.
- ○ The bees chew it.
- ○ The hexagonal shape of the hive makes it thick.

4 Sequence these steps as they happen in the text.
Write 1 to 4 in the boxes.

- ☐ Bees chew on the nectar to turn it into honey.
- ☐ The honeybee collects nectar from flowers.
- ☐ Worker bees suck out the nectar from the honey sac.
- ☐ Worker bees build tiny cells made of wax.

5 List two adjectives that have been used to describe the honey.

Remember, adjectives are describing words.

________________ ________________

BOB time!

UNIT 11

ADVANCED LEVEL

NARRATIVE TEXT: ADVENTURE STORY

A **narrative** is a story that is written to entertain the audience. It can use emotions such as fear, sadness or happiness to engage the reader. Often the story will be told with details of the events and characters to make it more interesting.

Shipwrecked!

It was just after lunch when the boat started to sink.

The crew had started their journey early on a beautiful summer's day. It was the weekend, and no one had a care in the world. Rocco and Brice were aiming to catch a few fish for dinner out in the bay, and the girls were hoping to dive off the boat and go for a swim.

Then disaster struck. With no warning at all, water began gushing into the boat from the floor. A panel of wood had split in two as easily as takeaway chopsticks. The boys rushed to collect the water in their hands and throw it overboard while Chloe and Anna used the fishing bucket, but it was no use. The water was coming in much faster than they could get rid of it.

Their father quickly took control before panic could set in. He ordered the kids to make sure their life jackets were secure. The boat was going down and there was nothing they could do about it. The children made a mad dash to grab their things but Dad said there was no point. They wouldn't be able to swim while holding onto their things.

The water was far colder than they expected. Silently, as they huddled together in the water, they watched the boat go down, swallowed up by the deep, mysterious sea. Dad shed a quiet tear as the last tip of his boat went under …

WORD BANK

crew a group of people who work together on a ship or plane

disaster a sudden event that causes suffering and damage

gushing when a large amount of liquid flows forcefully

We practise

Adverbial phrases do the same work as adverbs. They describe actions and add information about how, when, where, why or for how long things happen:

With no warning at all
Before panic could set in
as they huddled together in the water

Read Shipwrecked! and answer the questions.

Shade ONE bubble in questions 1 to 4.

1 What was the purpose of the boat trip?

- ○ to test the boat
- ○ to go swimming and fishing in the bay
- ○ to get from one bay to another
- ○ to go crabbing

What did the characters want to do while on the boat?

2 Who is telling the story?

- ○ Dad
- ○ Chloe
- ○ the narrator
- ○ Rocco

3 What does the narrator mean by 'no one had a care in the world'?

- ○ Everyone was scared.
- ○ No one cared about the world.
- ○ People forgot about their worries when they were on the boat.
- ○ No one had a car.

What is another word with the same meaning as 'care'?

4 Which one is an example of personification?

- ○ panic set in
- ○ then disaster struck
- ○ swallowed up by the deep, mysterious sea
- ○ water began gushing

Remember, personification is when a human nature or form is given to something.

5 Write down a simile used in this text.

You have finished the advanced reading level. Now try the reading tests on pages 34–36. Good luck!

BOB time!

BEGINNER LEVEL

READING TEST 1

NARRATIVE TEXT

Use 2B or HB pencil only.
Time limit: 8 minutes

Read the adventure story **James and the creature from the creek** on page 2 of the pull-out Reading and Writing Test Booklet, then answer questions 1 to 6.

Shade ONE bubble in questions 1 to 5.

1 Why did James go looking for yabbies?

- ○ He ate yabbies every day.
- ○ He wanted to cook them for his lunch.
- ○ He was looking for a creature to play with.
- ○ He was curious.

2 Why did James have trouble getting his words out?

- ○ He was trying to sound scary to the creek creature.
- ○ He was scared.
- ○ He was shivering with cold.
- ○ The creature wouldn't let him talk.

3 Why did James climb on the creature's back?

- ○ He was bored.
- ○ He was scared.
- ○ He was curious.
- ○ He was tough.

4 Why was James never bored again?

- ○ There was plenty to do in Nowheresville.
- ○ He played with all of his friends.
- ○ The creature from the creek took James on lots of adventures.
- ○ There were lots of yabbies to catch in the creek.

5 What does the narrator mean by James being curious? Shade ONE bubble.

- ○ He was adventurous.
- ○ He was nosy.
- ○ He was clever.
- ○ He was careful.

6 Order these sentences as they happen in the story. Write 1 to 4 in the boxes.

- ☐ James hopped on the creek creature's back.
- ☐ James thought he was hearing things.
- ☐ James went looking for yabbies in the creek.
- ☐ James heard a very low voice calling his name.

BOB time!

Use 2B or HB pencil only.
Time limit: 8 minutes

READING TEST 2

INFORMATION TEXT

BEGINNER LEVEL

Read the explanation **Cow chow** on page 2 of the pull-out Reading and Writing Test Booklet, then answer questions 1 to 6.

Shade ONE bubble in questions 1 to 5.

1 Where do cows live?

- ○ in the forest
- ○ in paddocks on farms
- ○ in warm areas
- ○ near trees

2 What is a ruminant animal?

- ○ an animal with a rumen
- ○ a farm animal
- ○ an animal that partly digests its food and then chews it again
- ○ an animal that eats grains

3 A cow's stomach is divided into

- ○ four different parts known as cuds.
- ○ three different parts.
- ○ four different parts called rumens.
- ○ four stomachs.

4 How many other animal species are ruminants?

- ○ goats, camels and giraffes
- ○ only farm animals
- ○ about 150
- ○ about 200

5 This text could also be called

- ○ Milking cows.
- ○ How a cow sleeps.
- ○ Farm animals.
- ○ Ruminant animals.

6 Put these sentences in the right order. Write 1 to 4 in the boxes.

- ☐ The cow chews the food and swallows it.
- ☐ The cud mixes with the saliva.
- ☐ Later on, the cow brings the food up and chews it again.
- ☐ The farmer gives the cow some grains and hay.

BOB time!

BEGINNER LEVEL

READING TEST 3

NARRATIVE TEXT

Use 2B or HB pencil only.
Time limit: 8 minutes

Read the poem **The worst class in the school** on page 3 of the pull-out Reading and Writing Test Booklet, then answer questions 1 to 6.

Shade ONE bubble in questions 1 to 5.

1 'A sideshow of circus clowns' probably means

- ⬭ the kids are at the circus.
- ⬭ the kids are laughing and being silly in class.
- ⬭ the teacher is really a clown.
- ⬭ the children are at the Royal Show.

2 Who lined up at the door?

- ⬭ lions
- ⬭ the class
- ⬭ hyenas
- ⬭ the teacher

3 Who made the sound 'like a gunshot' on the board?

- ⬭ the girls
- ⬭ the boys
- ⬭ the teacher
- ⬭ a clown

4 Who said the last line of the poem?

- ⬭ the kids in the back row
- ⬭ the teacher
- ⬭ the giggling girls
- ⬭ the boys who threw paper planes

5 What line below tells you that the classroom was a mess?

- ⬭ a sudden bang on the board
- ⬭ the girls giggling like a gaggle of geese
- ⬭ laughing rudely like screeching hyenas
- ⬭ schoolbooks scattered on the floor

6 Write a simile from this poem.

____

BOB time!

Use 2B or HB pencil only.
Time limit: 8 minutes

READING TEST 4

PERSUASIVE TEXT

MEDIUM LEVEL

Read the exposition **Save every drop** on page 3 of the pull-out Reading and Writing Test Booklet, then answer questions 1 to 6.

Shade ONE bubble in questions 1 to 5.

1 What is the problem in this text?

- ○ We are running out of fresh water.
- ○ We are using fresh water faster than it can be replaced.
- ○ The water supply has dried up.
- ○ The oceans are getting smaller.

2 What is the main point that the author is trying to make?

- ○ Drink more water.
- ○ Save as much water as possible.
- ○ Stop using water.
- ○ Stop washing ourselves.

3 Which one of these is not in the text?

- ○ Water is needed to provide power.
- ○ Saving water can save us money.
- ○ We need to use water wisely.
- ○ Ocean water is good for drinking.

4 Which words below are persuasive words?

- ○ water, saving, easy
- ○ fresh, faster, fix
- ○ need, must, should
- ○ money, soap, dishwasher

5 Who do you think this text is written for?

- ○ adults
- ○ children
- ○ people with no water
- ○ people at the Water Authority

6 Does the author present another point of view?

____

MEDIUM LEVEL

READING TEST 5

INFORMATION TEXT

Use 2B or HB pencil only.
Time limit: 8 minutes

Read the procedure **Measuring your height** on page 4 of the pull-out Reading and Writing Test Booklet, then answer questions 1 to 6.

Shade ONE bubble in questions 1 to 4.

1 What is the first thing you need to do?

- ○ Sit down.
- ○ Get the things that you need.
- ○ Measure the wall.
- ○ Take your shoes off.

2 Why is another person needed for this?

- ○ to mark the wall at the correct height
- ○ to check you are doing it right
- ○ to keep you company
- ○ to tell jokes

3 How many steps are there to this procedure?

- ○ 5
- ○ 6
- ○ 7
- ○ 8

4 Why do you think a tape measure is used?

- ○ You would have to keep moving the ruler to reach the mark.
- ○ A tape measure is the easiest way to measure the total height.
- ○ If you used a ruler, the height might not be exact after all of the moving.
- ○ all of the above

5 Order these steps as they happen in the text. Write 1 to 5 in the boxes.

- ☐ Use a tape measure to measure the total height.
- ☐ Use a book or ruler to help mark the wall.
- ☐ Take your shoes off.
- ☐ Convert the centimetres to metres.
- ☐ Stand up straight against a wall.

6 What step comes straight after marking the wall?

____

____

____

____

____

____

____

BOB time!

Use 2B or HB pencil only.
Time limit: 8 minutes

READING TEST 6

INFORMATION TEXT

MEDIUM LEVEL

Read the explanation **What is a 'falling star'?** on page 4 of the pull-out Reading and Writing Test Booklet, then answer questions 1 to 6.

Shade ONE bubble in questions 1 to 4.

1 A shooting star is really

- ○ an exploding star.
- ○ a star with a gun.
- ○ a streak of light.
- ○ a comet.

2 Why is it harder to see meteors during the day?

- ○ They are usually smaller than a pebble.
- ○ They only happen at night.
- ○ It's easier to see a light at night than in the daytime.
- ○ The sun is in the way.

3 What is the second paragraph about?

- ○ meteoroids burning up in the atmosphere
- ○ falling stars in the sky
- ○ asteroids
- ○ meteorites

4 What else could this text be called?

- ○ About meteoroids
- ○ The Earth's atmosphere
- ○ Exploding stars
- ○ Comets in the sky

5 Sequence these events from the text. Write 1 to 4 in the boxes.

- ☐ A star appears to fall in the sky.
- ☐ A glow forms.
- ☐ A tiny particle enters the Earth's atmosphere.
- ☐ It burns up.

BOB time!

Is this statement true or false? Write your answer on the line.

6 A meteoroid is a glow of light. ____________________

ADVANCED LEVEL

READING TEST 7

NARRATIVE TEXT

Use 2B or HB pencil only.
Time limit: 8 minutes

Read the traditional story **How the kiwi lost its wings** on page 5 of the pull-out Reading and Writing Test Booklet, then answer questions 1 to 6.

Shade ONE bubble in questions 1 to 5.

1 Who was Tane-mahuta?

- ○ the god of the children
- ○ the god of the forest
- ○ the god of the birds
- ○ the god of the kiwis

2 Who was Tane-hokohoka's brother?

- ○ Tui
- ○ Tane-mahuta
- ○ Pukeko
- ○ Pipiwharauroa

3 What else does this myth explain?

- ○ how the kiwi got a long beak
- ○ why the kiwi likes the rain
- ○ how the kiwi got an excuse
- ○ how the kiwi got strong legs

4 Why do you think the other birds had excuses?

- ○ They didn't want to live on the forest floor.
- ○ They were mean.
- ○ They were sick.
- ○ They wanted to live in the ocean.

5 How did the god of the forest thank the kiwi?

- ○ He made him the chief of the forest.
- ○ He gave him beautiful feathers.
- ○ He made him the most popular bird.
- ○ He gave him strong legs.

6 By living on the forest floor, how did the kiwi help the god of the forest?

____

BOB time!

Use 2B or HB pencil only.
Time limit: 8 minutes

READING TEST 8

PERSUASIVE TEXT

ADVANCED LEVEL

Read the advertisement **The Lunar Zoomer** on page 5 of the pull-out Reading and Writing Test Booklet, then answer questions 1 to 6.

Shade ONE bubble in questions 1 to 5.

1 What is the Lunar Zoomer?

- ○ a ride at the Royal Show
- ○ a spacecraft
- ○ a jet plane
- ○ a ship

2 What does a ticket cost on the Lunar Zoomer?

- ○ a thousand dollars
- ○ a million dollars
- ○ a hundred dollars
- ○ ten dollars

3 Who is organising these trips?

- ○ the hostesses
- ○ Moon Voyages
- ○ the Lunar Zoomer
- ○ the pilot

4 How can you get a ticket for this flight?

- ○ you have to win a ticket
- ○ call 13 MOON
- ○ email the Lunar Zoomer
- ○ visit the moon

5 The purpose of this advertisement is to

- ○ show you what moon seats look like.
- ○ make you book a ticket today.
- ○ tell you about moon snacks.
- ○ tell you how the Lunar Zoomer works.

6 What is the purpose of the images in this advertisement?

____

ADVANCED LEVEL

READING TEST 9

INFORMATION TEXT

Use 2B or HB pencil only.
Time limit: 8 minutes

Read the report **Vietnamese New Year** on page 6 of the pull-out Reading and Writing Test Booklet, then answer questions 1 to 6.

1 **When is Vietnamese New Year celebrated?** ______________________________

Shade ONE bubble in questions 2 to 5.

2 **Why is the first visitor to the house so important?**

- ○ It is their birthday.
- ○ They can make everyone happy.
- ○ They bring money.
- ○ They can bring good luck for the year.

3 **The Tet celebration is based on**

- ○ the months.
- ○ the Sun.
- ○ the stars.
- ○ the Moon.

4 **How is Tet different to the normal calendar New Year?**

- ○ People visit other people during Tet.
- ○ There are lots of celebrations.
- ○ During Tet it is everybody's birthday.
- ○ The parks are full of people.

5 **The third paragraph is mainly about**

- ○ incense.
- ○ the celebrations during Tet.
- ○ visitors.
- ○ birthdays.

6 **What sorts of visitors do people like to have during Tet? Why?**

____

____

TIPS for NAPLAN* WRITING

Audience

* Use a catchy title.
  Example: Instead of *Waterfalls*, try *The Wonders of Waterfalls*.
* Write to inform but keep it interesting!

Structure

* Have an introduction, body and conclusion.
* Include lots of facts and details.
* The introduction needs to clearly say what you are writing about.

Ideas

* Include interesting ideas or features, and be clear when explaining something.

Description and details (informative writing)

* Use similes to compare things.
  Example: *as tall as, as heavy as*
* Provide reasons for things wherever you can.
  Example: Instead of '*some birds can fly and some can't*', use '*some birds cannot fly because they are too large*'.

Character and setting (narrative writing)

* Include where and when the story is taking place.
* Use figurative language in narratives to provide more details.
  Example: Instead of '*he was hungry*', try '*he was as hungry as a lion in a flower patch*'.

Persuasive devices (persuasive writing)

* Use expert opinions to back up your argument.
  Example: *Doctor Les Makeyouwell reports that chocolate should be eaten at least once a day.*

Vocabulary

* Try to use interesting and specific words.
* Use synonyms and figurative language.
  Example: If the topic is insects, then use '*these tiny winged creatures*' and '*the small six-legged beasts*', instead of using the word '*insects*' all the time.

Cohesion

* Don't overuse the words *and* and *then*.
* Your details and ideas should flow on from each other.
* Link your sentences' ideas together using words such as *however, although* and *to begin with*.

Paragraphs

* Each paragraph should have one idea and some sentences to back up that idea.
* Don't repeat something you have already written.

Sentence structure

* Try to create complex sentences. These sentences have two or three details in them.
  Example: Instead of '*He liked eating popcorn. He was skinny.*', use, '*Although he liked eating a lot of popcorn, he was still fairly skinny*'.

Punctuation

* Use speech in stories, as it is a good way to show your understanding of punctuation.
* In persuasive and informative texts, remember to use contractions.
  Example: *didn't, couldn't, shouldn't*

Spelling

* Mainly use words that you know how to spell, but it's also OK to try words you aren't too sure of.

*This is not an officially endorsed publication of the NAPLAN program and is produced by Pascal Press independently of Australian Governments.

UNIT 12

NARRATIVE WRITING: ADVENTURE STORY

The purpose of narrative writing is to entertain the reader.

There are many different types of narratives. These include myths and legends, poetry, science fiction, mystery, real life stories, fables, fairy and folk tales, horror and historical stories.

Narrative:

* Told from your point of view (first person)
  Example: *I hid under the bed, shaking with fear!*
* May be told as if you were watching it happen (third person)
  Example: *The boy ran as fast as he could to get away from the fire.*
* Many are imaginative texts — usually a problem (complication) needs to be solved
* May use humour or emotions, such as suspense, anger or sadness
* Uses lots of descriptive language

Planning a narrative:

Beginning (Orientation)

* Introduces the main characters without too much detail — more is explained as the narrative unfolds
* Talks about where and when the story took place (setting)
* Sets the scene for the 'complication'

Middle (Complication)

* Talks about the complication of the story — where something goes wrong and needs to be fixed or solved
  Example: *In* Little Red Riding Hood, *the complication is when the Big Bad Wolf eats Grandmother and tries to trick Little Red Riding Hood.*
* Sometimes has more than one complication

Ending (Resolution)

* Where the complication is solved, usually by the main character
* Lesson or moral to the story is written here

Use the title to create interest. It should also match your story.

A good introduction is important. Hook the reader in by making them want to find out more about where the story is headed.

Even if you can't spell a word, have a go as it will help with your vocabulary and make your story more exciting.

When describing characters, focus on appearance, personality and background.

Be careful with your punctuation, especially when it comes to speech.

Try to use figurative language to help with descriptions of things and events.

Make sure your narrative flows on and that the events follow on using interesting sentences. Try to avoid using 'next' and 'then'.

ALWAYS take time to re-read and edit your work. You may be so busy thinking about an idea that you forget to actually include it in your story!

Analysis of sample adventure story text

Wee Bob Roy

Describes where and when the story took place.

The beginning introduces the main character.

BEGINNING

Many years ago, a young man went on a journey to a faraway land. He travelled through the city and saw plenty of amazing scenes. He was very impressed with what he saw.

Uses lots of adjectives to describe places and things

The middle section has a complication and creates interest.

MIDDLE

"Who designed this wonderful building?" he asked a passer-by, as he pointed to a magnificent castle. It was as splendid as the crown jewels themselves.

"Wee Bob Roy," replied the stranger.

Later, he was visiting an art gallery and he saw some brilliant paintings that looked directly at him.

"Who painted these stunning pictures?" he asked the gallery owner.

The owner told him, "Wee Bob Roy".

The curious traveller thought that this Wee Bob Roy must be very talented indeed.

That evening he walked past a gorgeous garden of gerberas. It was a canvas of colour, calling out to him.

"Who created this amazing garden of gerberas?" the man asked.

"Wee Bob Roy," a woman told him as she brushed past him.

"I have to meet this mysterious Wee Bob Roy," the traveller decided.

Uses figurative language such as similes, alliteration, metaphors and personification

Uses synonyms to avoid using the same words. Instead of gorgeous uses amazing, stunning, brilliant, splendid and magnificent.

The ending brings the story together and ties up any loose ends.

ENDING

The next day the man bought a phrasebook to help learn the language of the land. The first phrase he saw was how to say, "I don't understand". And right next to it were the words "Wee Bob Roy".

NARRATIVE

Adventure story worksheet

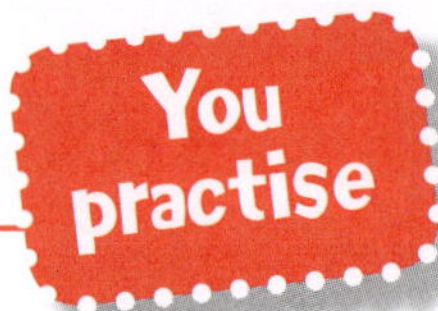

NARRATIVE

An adjective is a describing word. It describes the colour, size, number or feel of something.

Underline the adjectives.

 1 two small, pink flowers

 2 a narrow, winding path

 3 three tall, pointy towers

Underline the adjectives in each sentence.

 4 A young man went on a journey to a faraway land.

 5 He saw plenty of amazing scenes.

6 Who designed this wonderful building?

Using different adjectives, synonyms, makes your writing interesting. Write an adjective that has the same meaning as these ones.

Example: *huge* enormous

7 tiny ______________________

 8 skinny ______________________

 9 horrible ______________________

Write a noun to match these adjectives.

Example: *tall, thin, black* tree trunk

 10 small, brown, slimy ______________________

 11 enormous, green, wet ______________________

 12 hard, cold, grey ______________________

BOB time!

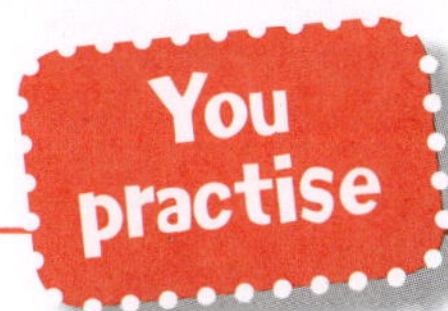

Adventure story planning sheet

Use this sheet to write a story with the title below. The pictures will help you brainstorm ideas for your writing.

NARRATIVE

Title: The weirdest day EVER!

Beginning

Setting (where and when the story takes place): ______

Characters: ______

Middle

This is where the action takes place. Introduce the 'complication' or problem to your story. ______

What are some describing words you might use? Think of some synonyms for 'weird'.

______

What else happens in your story? ______

Ending

How does your story end? Is there a lesson to be learned? ______

Now turn to the next page and write your own narrative. Use the marking checklist so you don't miss anything.

Adventure story marking checklist

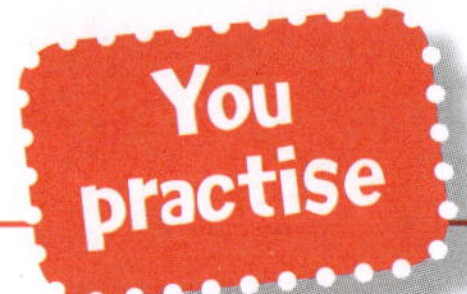

Before your child begins to write, read through the marking checklist as a reminder of what needs to be included. When your child has finished writing, give them a mark for each criterion.

Criteria	Assessment	Yes	No	Mark
Audience *(0–6 marks)*	o Does the title match the story? o Does the story entertain and engage the reader? o Have narrative devices been used (e.g. humour, emotion)?			
Structure *(0–4 marks)*	o Are the events in the story detailed? o Is there a clear complication? o Does the conclusion resolve the problem? o Is there a twist at the end?			
Ideas *(0–5 marks)*	o Is there a central theme (e.g. good versus evil)? o Is there detail in the events of the story?			
Character and setting *(0–4 marks)*	o Is there a setting in the introduction? o Has dialogue been included? o Have good descriptions of main characters been given?			
Vocabulary *(0–4 marks)*	o Have relevant and concise words been used? o Does the vocabulary match the narrative genre? o Has figurative language been used (e.g. metaphor, personification, simile)? o Is the writing fluent and articulate?			
Cohesion *(0–4 marks)*	o Have ideas been linked correctly? o Is the story easy for the reader to follow? o Has a range of linking words (e.g. meanwhile, because, after, since) been used? o Have synonyms been used?			
Paragraphs *(0–3 marks)*	o Are the paragraphs sequenced properly? o Does each paragraph focus on one idea or event?			
Sentence structure *(0–6 marks)*	o Are the grammatical structures of the sentences correct? o Have complex sentences been used?			
Punctuation *(0–5 marks)*	o Have capitals, commas, apostrophes, full stops and quotation marks been used correctly?			
Spelling *(0–6 marks)*	o Are there more words spelled correctly than incorrectly? o Have challenging words been used?			

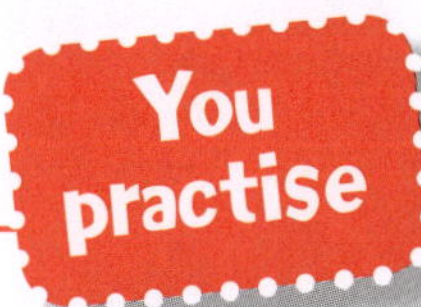

Adventure story writing exercise

The weirdest day EVER!

Now try the narrative writing test on page 8 of the Reading and Writing Test Booklet.

UNIT 13

INFORMATIVE WRITING: FACTUAL RECOUNT

The purpose of recount writing is to describe a series of events in the same order as they happened. A recount might be **personal** (like a diary entry), **factual** (like a news report) or **imaginary** (as part of a narrative).

Recount:

- Told from your point of view (first person)
  Example: *First we went to the supermarket.*
- May be told as if you were watching it happen (third person)
  Example: *The boy ran as fast as he could.*
- Follows a sequence of events and may include personal opinions, emotions and feelings
- Uses lots of descriptive language

Planning a recount:

Introduction

- Opening paragraph usually sets the scene
- Tells us *who, what, when, where* and *why*

Body

- Recounts the events in order
- Follows a sequence — paragraphs may need to use **connectives** such as *after that, as a result, this is because, following that* and *so on*
- Always uses past tense to recount events
  Example: *We went there and did that.*

Conclusion

- Draws the events to a close
- Adds personal opinion

Give your recount a clear title. Instead of The Zoo, use Our Trip to the Zoo or The Zoo Excursion.

Use the first paragraph to introduce the subject and to explain any key words.

Sequence your writing carefully so the events flow.

Create interest with exclamations or observations, e.g. Beware – Bushfires can kill!

Finish by adding a summing up sentence in a concluding paragraph.

Analysis of sample factual recount

The dentist visit

Describes where and when the story took place.

INTRODUCTION

The introduction sets the scene.

On the weekend, one of my new adult teeth started to really hurt, so on Monday afternoon I had a horror visit to the dentist. My mum took me, and I was glad she was there because I needed someone to hold my hand.

Describes who, what and why

Uses personal pronouns

BODY

The body recounts the events in order.

First of all, the dentist looked in my mouth and said, "OH NO!"

When I heard that, it really freaked me out. Before I had a chance to think, he said he was going to give me a needle. YES – a needle!

Uses past tense to recount events

Following the shock of the needle, I noticed that everything suddenly went numb. This wasn't so bad, except the scary dentist kept asking me questions!

It was very hard to talk with the numbness, so I just nodded my head to let him know.

Orders and links the events using connectives to create cohesion

The next thing I knew, a drill was turned on and the noise was deafening, like loud thunder in a storm. Thankfully, I couldn't feel anything, but the sight of the drill was enough to make me feel dizzy.

Uses figurative language to add detail, e.g. simile

DENTIST

As a result, my mum had to sing some of my favorite lullabies from when I was a baby to calm me down. It was so embarrassing!

Uses lots of adjectives (describing words)

CONCLUSION

The conclusion draws the events to a close.

Finally, the crazy dentist told me it was all over. He asked me to rinse out my mouth with this disgusting pink liquid. I was then told that I couldn't eat anything chewy for a while. I managed to blurt out, "Thacks for fickthing my thooth."

Factual recount worksheet

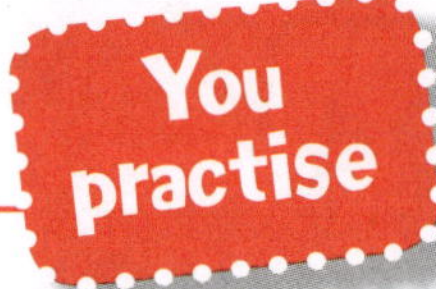

INFORMATIVE

The tense of a verb tells you when the action is taking place.
There are 3 main tenses: present, past and future.

Present tense – tells you what is happening now.
*My mum always **takes** me to the dentist.*

Past tense – tells you what has already happened.
*The dentist **looked** in my mouth.*

Future tense – tells you what will happen in the future.
*He **will give** me a needle.*

In recount writing we use the past tense.

Underline the verb in each sentence.

1 Sam waits for her mum by the school gate every day.

2 Yesterday her mum got a new job.

3 Sam will ride home on her bike from now on.

Choose the correct verb tense to complete each sentence. Write it in the box.

4 The dentist *is putting / put* a filling in my tooth last time. [ ]

5 Now I *brush / brushed* my teeth three times a day! [ ]

6 Mum *takes / will take* me back to the dentist next year. [ ]

Write the verbs from the box on the correct lines.

will tell	*asked*	*looks*	*heard*	*is nodding*	*will notice*

7 Present tense ____________ ____________

8 Past tense ____________ ____________

9 Future tense ____________ ____________

You practise

Factual recount planning sheet

UNIT 13

Use this sheet to write a recount with the title below. The pictures will help you brainstorm ideas for your writing.

INFORMATIVE

Title: The first day of school

Introduction

Where and when: ____________________

Explain who, what and why: ____________________

Middle

Write the events here and then work out how you will connect them up to flow in sequence. This is known as 'cohesion'. ____________________

Conclusion

How does it all end? You can add your opinion. ____________________

Now turn to the next page and write your own recount. Use the marking checklist so you don't miss anything.

Factual recount marking checklist

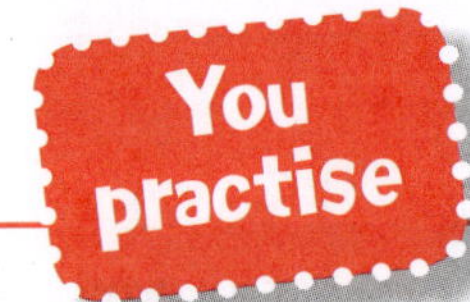

INFORMATIVE

Before your child begins to write, read through the marking checklist as a reminder of what needs to be included. When your child has finished writing, give them a mark for each criterion.

Criteria	Assessment	Yes	No	Mark
Audience *(0–6 marks)*	o Does the title clearly explain what the text is about? o Is it easy for the reader to follow and understand? o Is there detail at different stages of the recount? o Does the text engage the reader well?			
Structure *(0–4 marks)*	o Is there an introduction, a body and a conclusion? o Are the three sections separate and well developed? o Have details been included at different stages of the events?			
Ideas *(0–5 marks)*	o Are the ideas relevant? o Is there enough detail for each idea? o Is the topic explained coherently?			
Description and details *(0–4 marks)*	o Have lots of adjectives been used to add detail? o Are examples and reasons provided? o Is the explanation clear?			
Vocabulary *(0–4 marks)*	o Have relevant and concise words been used? o Is the writing fluent and articulate?			
Cohesion *(0–4 marks)*	o Have ideas been linked correctly? o Is it easy for the reader to follow? o Has a range of linking words (e.g. meanwhile, because, after, since) been used? o Have synonyms been used?			
Paragraphs *(0–3 marks)*	o Are the paragraphs well organised? o Do they have a topic sentence with supporting details?			
Sentence structure *(0–6 marks)*	o Are the grammatical structures of the sentences correct? o Have complex sentences been used?			
Punctuation *(0–5 marks)*	o Have capitals, commas, apostrophes, full stops and quotation marks been used correctly?			
Spelling *(0–6 marks)*	o Are there more words spelled correctly than incorrectly? o Have challenging words been used?			

You practise

Factual recount writing exercise

The first day of school

UNIT 13

INFORMATIVE

Now try the recount writing test on page 10 of the Reading and Writing Test Booklet.

INFORMATIVE WRITING: EXPLANATION

The purpose of informative writing is to provide information on a topic.
It may include why something occurs or how something works (an **explanation**) or the features and facts of a topic.

Explanation:

* May start with a question
  Example: *Have you ever wondered why an emu cannot fly?*
* Written to inform and provide facts on a topic
* Uses technical words
* May give a number of reasons **why** something happens
* May follow a sequence of stages in a process
* Does not contain personal opinions or stories about the topic

Planning an explanation:

Introduction

* A general opening statement that may be a question
* An outline of the topic and some background information that might answer who, what, when, where and why

Body

* Contains a series of paragraphs that each deal with a different part of the topic
* Has paragraphs that follow the stages or steps in the process being explained
* Follows a sequence — the paragraphs may need to use **connectives** such as *after that, and so on, as a result, this is because* and *although*

Conclusion

* Does not present any new information
* Brings all the ideas together

Decide if your explanation might need a diagram or chart to explain your topic.

Create interest with exclamations or observations, e.g. Beware – Bushfires can kill!

Give your text a clear title. Instead of Rainbows, use Why Do Rainbows Occur?

Use the first paragraph to introduce the subject and to define any key words.

Re-read your explanation, pretending that you do not know anything about the subject. Does it make sense?

Finish by drawing your ideas together in a concluding paragraph.

Organise your writing carefully. Do the ideas and points flow?

We practise

Analysis of sample explanation text

How clouds are formed

The title clearly states what the text is going to explain.

INTRODUCTION

Have you ever wondered what clouds are made of? Some of them look like gigantic balls of cotton wool; however, clouds are actually made from water. The way they are formed is a very interesting process.

The introduction may ask a question to create interest.

INFORMATIVE

BODY

Basically, a cloud is a large collection of very tiny droplets of water and ice crystals. Because the droplets are so small and light, they can float in the air.

The way that clouds form is part of the water cycle. Air contains water no matter how hot or cold it is. The water in the air near the ground is usually in a gas form and cannot be seen. It is known as water vapour.

In the first stage of the cycle, the sun shines down and makes the ground warm. This then causes the warm air to rise up into cooler parts. As the warm air rises, it expands and also cools down. This process is known as evaporation.

The cool air is not able to hold water as well as water vapour and, as a result, some of it condenses onto particles of dust that are floating in the air. When this happens, a tiny droplet forms around each particle. This process is known as condensation.

The body follows stages or steps in the process.

Includes a diagram to show a process

Defines any technical terms

Uses connectives to link a sequence

CONCLUSION

Clouds are formed when millions, in fact even billions, of these dust droplets join up together. Sometimes they form a rain cloud, which means the water will eventually drop down to the ground so that the process can start over.

The conclusion brings everything together.

Explanation worksheet

Vocabulary for informative writing

When you write to inform another person about a topic you have to use special words.

These are often factual or technical words.

Example: make = *build, construct, produce, assemble*

You will also need to use words that join or link your ideas.

Example: *although, firstly, finally*

Write the technical word from the box next to the simple word that it matches.

mature	*habitat*	*explore*	*search*	*shelter*
investigate	*safe haven*	*produce*	*develop*	

1. home ____________ ____________ ____________

2. look for ____________ ____________ ____________

3. grow ____________ ____________ ____________

4. **Choose linking words from the box to complete the gaps.**
   Hint: There are more words than you need.

as	*then*	*although*	*firstly*	*because*	*as a result*

____________, the sun shines down and makes the ground warm. The warm air ____________ rises up into cooler parts. As the warm air rises, it cools down and expands. The cool air is not able to hold water as well as water vapour. ____________, some of it condenses.

BOB time!

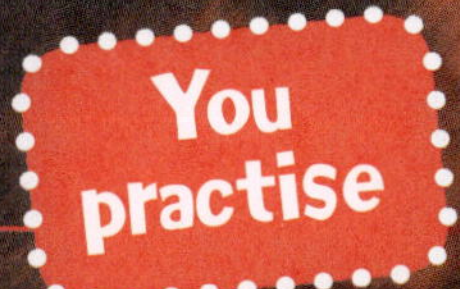

Explanation planning sheet

Use this sheet to write an explanation with the title below. The pictures will help you brainstorm ideas for your writing.

INFORMATIVE

Title: How do bushfires start?

Introduction

I will be explaining why ______________________________

____

Write a starting sentence. Example: *Did you know that just one tiny flicker of a flame can start a massive bushfire?* ______________________________

____

Body

There are several reasons for this. The main reason is ______________________________

____

____

Another reason is ______________________________

____

A further reason is ______________________________

____

Conclusion

Write a finishing sentence. Example: *So now you can see how bushfires* ______________________________

____

____

Now turn to the next page and write your own explanation. Use the marking checklist so you don't miss anything.

Explanation marking checklist

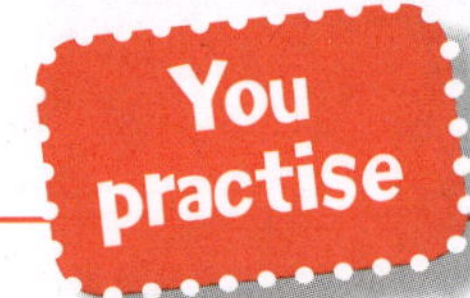

Before your child begins to write, read through the marking checklist as a reminder of what needs to be included. When your child has finished writing, give them a mark for each criterion.

Criteria	Assessment	Yes	No	Mark
Audience *(0–6 marks)*	o Does the title clearly explain what the text is about? o Is it easy for the reader to follow and understand? o Is there detail at different stages of the explanation? o Does the text engage the reader well?			
Structure *(0–4 marks)*	o Is there an introduction, a body and a conclusion? o Are the three sections separate and well developed? o Have details been included at different stages of the events?			
Ideas *(0–5 marks)*	o Are the ideas relevant? o Is there enough detail for each idea? o Is the topic explained coherently?			
Description and details *(0–4 marks)*	o Have lots of adjectives been used to add detail? o Are examples and reasons provided? o Is the explanation clear?			
Vocabulary *(0–4 marks)*	o Have relevant and concise words been used? o Is the writing fluent and articulate?			
Cohesion *(0–4 marks)*	o Have ideas been linked correctly? o Is it easy for the reader to follow? o Has a range of linking words (e.g. meanwhile, because, after, since) been used? o Have synonyms been used?			
Paragraphs *(0–3 marks)*	o Are the paragraphs well organised? o Do they have a topic sentence with supporting details?			
Sentence structure *(0–6 marks)*	o Are the grammatical structures of the sentences correct? o Have complex sentences been used?			
Punctuation *(0–5 marks)*	o Have capitals, commas, apostrophes, full stops and quotation marks been used correctly?			
Spelling *(0–6 marks)*	o Are there more words spelled correctly than incorrectly? o Have challenging words been used?			

You practise

UNIT 14

Explanation writing exercise

How do bushfires start?

Now try the explanation writing test on page 12 of the Reading and Writing Test Booklet.

UNIT 15

PERSUASIVE WRITING: EXPOSITION

The purpose of persuasive writing is to get across an opinion or point of view on a particular topic.

Persuasive texts include **expositions** where only one side of an argument is presented. Other types of persuasive texts include **advertisements** and **discussions** or **debates** on a topic.

Exposition:

- Usually presents only one side of an argument
- Are biased and try to sound correct to help convince the reader to share the same view
  Example: *School should start at 10 am.*

Discussion:

- Might look at a difficult topic that has many sides to it
- Needs to be convincing
- Tries to weigh up all sides of the story
  Example: *Should animals be hunted?*

Planning a persuasive exposition:

Introduction

- Clearly states your opinion
- Includes an outline of the important argument that the text will cover
- May have some background information

Body

- Presents the argument points clearly
- Orders the paragraphs using words such as *firstly*, *secondly* and *finally*
- Uses persuasive words such as *please, should, must, will, need, save, fight* and *take*
- Does not go off the topic and sticks to the points of the argument
- Might include reasons or examples to back up the argument
- Might use reports, quotes or evidence from 'experts'

Conclusion

- Sums up the main argument
- Does not present any new information
- May ask the reader to take action on the topic

Quote statistics and use them to support your argument.

Tell your reader what they would like to hear.

Use emotive or biased vocabulary such as obviously, clearly, surely.

Make an emotional appeal to your reader, e.g. If you believe that ..., then please ...

Use scientific facts and formulas, and technical words.

Analysis of sample exposition text

Chocolate is not junk food

The title clearly states what the text is about.

INTRODUCTION

The introduction states an opinion.

When we think of junk food, we think of foods that are not healthy. In my opinion, chocolate, especially dark chocolate, should not be called junk food as it can do many good things for our bodies.

BODY

The body clearly presents the argument points by ordering them.

Uses action words, persuasive words and feeling words.

Firstly, you may not know this, but chocolate is made from natural ingredients. Most junk foods have too much unhealthy stuff in them, like salt, fat and sugar. While chocolate does contain sugar, our bodies need some sugars to provide energy for us to play and work.

Includes facts to support the topic

Secondly, chocolate is made from cocoa beans, which are a natural substance. These beans contain *antioxidants*, which are very helpful to our bodies. Antioxidants can help prevent cancer and heart failure, and can also help our veins to work better. In fact, a chocolate bar has five times the amount of antioxidants than one apple.

Includes evidence based on research

Finally, I believe that eating chocolate can make us happy, which means less stress. Stress is not good for the body and will lead to all sorts of health problems.

CONCLUSION

The conclusion calls for action by asking the reader to 'grab' some chocolate.

So next time you need a healthy snack, grab a couple of pieces of dark chocolate and do your body a favour! You won't regret it.

Exposition worksheet

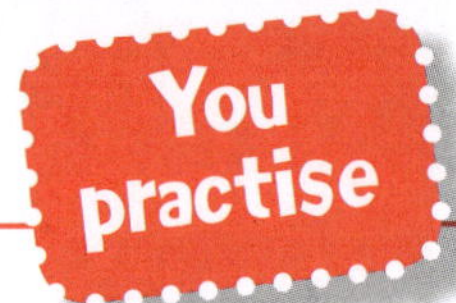

Emotive language

When you write to persuade another person to agree with your point of view, you need to use special words called emotive words.

These words are strong and can make us feel positive or negative.

PERSUASIVE

Sort these emotive words into the positive box or the negative box below.

wonderful	*incredible*	*conflict*	*confident*	*certain*	*annoy*
awful	*support*	*believe*	*punish*	*threaten*	*mistake*

Positive words	Negative words

Exposition planning sheet

Use this sheet to write a persuasive text with the title below.

Title: Zoos are more interesting than museums

Introduction

What your text will be about: ______________________

____

Main point

Do you agree or disagree that zoos are better than museums? Why? ______________________

____

____

First point

The most important point you will be making: ______________________

____

____

Example/s: ______________________

Second point

Other information you have to back up your argument: ______________________

____

____

Example/s: ______________________

Conclusion

Sum up your opinion and maybe include a call to action! ______________________

____

____

Now turn to the next page and write your own persuasive text. Use the marking checklist so you don't miss anything.

Exposition marking checklist

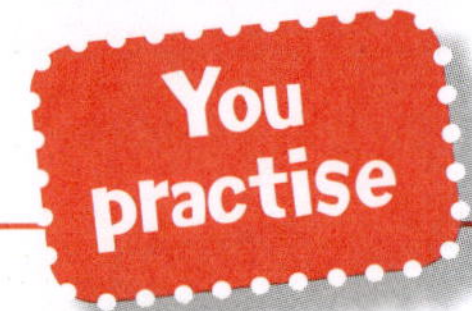

PERSUASIVE

Before your child begins to write, read through the marking checklist as a reminder of what needs to be included. When your child has finished writing, give them a mark for each criterion.

Criteria	Assessment	Yes	No	Mark
Audience *(0–6 marks)*	o Does the text contain reasons for arguments? o Is the information consistent? o Does the text engage the reader? o Have values been used to make a point?			
Structure *(0–4 marks)*	o Is there a clear introduction, a body and a conclusion? o Are 3–4 aspects of the topic included in the body? o Has detailed supporting evidence been included? o Does the conclusion clearly support the writer's view?			
Ideas *(0–5 marks)*	o Are there ideas other than personal opinion? o Are the ideas persuasive?			
Persuasive devices *(0–4 marks)*	o Do the ideas argue against the point of others? o Does the text appeal to values and emotions? o Have expert opinions been included?			
Vocabulary *(0–4 marks)*	o Have relevant and concise words been used? o Is the writing fluent and articulate?			
Cohesion *(0–4 marks)*	o Have ideas been linked correctly? o Is it easy for the reader to follow? o Has a range of linking words (e.g. meanwhile, because, after, since) been used? o Have synonyms been used?			
Paragraphs *(0–3 marks)*	o Are the paragraphs well organised? o Do they have a topic sentence with supporting details?			
Sentence structure *(0–6 marks)*	o Are the grammatical structures of the sentences correct? o Have complex sentences been used?			
Punctuation *(0–5 marks)*	o Have capitals, commas, apostrophes, full stops and quotation marks been used correctly?			
Spelling *(0–6 marks)*	o Are there more words spelled correctly than incorrectly? o Have challenging words been used?			

You practise

Exposition writing exercise

Zoos are more interesting than museums

Now try the persuasive writing test on page 14 of the Reading and Writing Test Booklet.

ANSWERS

Unit 1 – The ant and the grasshopper

1 gathering food
2 The ant is collecting food for winter.
3 He needs to store food for winter.
4 The ant wants to teach the grasshopper a lesson.
5 4,1,2,3

Unit 2 – Beautiful beetles

1 Features of beetles
2 oceans
3 Beetles come in different shapes and sizes.
4 head, thorax, abdomen
5 Their hard exoskeleton protects them from harm.

Unit 3 – Autumn days

1 an autumn scene
2 The leaves cover the ground like a carpet.
3 autumn leaves
4 It is behind clouds and fog.
5 Possible answers: red, orange, brown, crinkled, high, crisp, cool, low, dark, misty

Unit 4 – Book review by Jarrad

1 adventure
2 He really enjoyed it.
3 the two main characters
4 people who haven't read the book
5 The main characters are a girl and a boy.

Unit 5 – Lazy lamingtons

1 6
2 Sift icing sugar and cocoa together.
3 It allows the icing time to set.
4 It shows how the lamingtons should look when finished.
5 The sponge cake part is already made.

Unit 6 – How a snowflake is formed

1 the temperature at which the crystal forms
2 Snowflakes all have six arms.
3 temperature
4 4, 2, 3, 1
5 plate-like snowflake

Unit 7 – Picnic in the forest

1 They'd been planning it for weeks.
2 The group were very noisy.
3 Carla dropped some boiled eggs.
4 He had eaten too many sandwiches.
5 2, 1, 4, 3

Unit 8 – Tiddalik the frog

1 He was very thirsty.
2 They were cross.
3 the eel
4 They thought that they would never get their water back.
5 The kookaburra jumped over the emu.

Unit 9 – Recycle your rubbish!

1 It helps our planet.
2 people who are not recycling
3 There are no excuses for not recycling.
4 Recycling doesn't take up much time.
5 re-using shopping bags; buying refills for products

Unit 10 – How honey is made

1 how bees make honey
2 is where the bee stores the nectar.
3 The water in it evaporates.
4 4, 2, 3, 1
5 thick, sweet

Unit 11 – Shipwrecked!

1 to go swimming and fishing in the bay
2 the narrator
3 People forgot about their worries when they were on the boat.
4 swallowed up by the deep, mysterious sea
5 as easily as takeaway chopsticks

Reading test 1 – James and the creature from the creek

1 He wanted to cook them for his lunch.
2 He was scared.
3 He was curious.
4 The creature from the creek took James on lots of adventures.
5 He was adventurous.
6 4, 3, 1, 2

Reading test 2 – Cow chow

1 in paddocks on farms
2 an animal that partly digests its food and then chews it again
3 four different parts called rumens.
4 about 150
5 Ruminant animals
6 2, 4, 3, 1

Reading test 3 – The worst class in the school

1 Kids are laughing and being silly in class.
2 the class
3 the teacher
4 the teacher
5 schoolbooks scattered on the floor
6 crooked like an old man's walk; giggling like a gaggle of geese; like a gunshot in the street

Reading test 4 – Save every drop

1 We are using fresh water faster than it can be replaced.
2 Save as much water as possible.
3 Ocean water is good for drinking.
4 need, must, should
5 children
6 no

ANSWERS

Reading test 5 – Measuring your height

1. Take your shoes off.
2. to mark the wall at the correct height
3. 6
4. all of the above
5. 4, 3, 1, 5, 2
6. Place the tape measure with the 0 cm end at the floor to measure the height.

Reading test 6 – What is a 'falling star'?

1. a streak of light
2. It's easier to see a light at night than in the daytime.
3. meteoroids burning up in the atmosphere
4. About meteoroids
5. 4, 3, 1, 2
6. false

Reading test 7 – How the kiwi lost its wings

1. the god of the forest
2. Tane-mahuta
3. how the kiwi got strong legs
4. They didn't want to live on the forest floor.
5. He made him the most popular bird.
6. He tore apart the logs on the forest floor and stopped the trees from getting sick.

Reading test 8 – The Lunar Zoomer

1. a spacecraft
2. a million dollars
3. Moon Voyages
4. call 13 MOON
5. make you book a ticket today.
6. to encourage you to buy a ticket by showing you what you will be able to see

Reading test 9 – Vietnamese New Year

1. the first morning of the first day of the new period OR around late January and early February
2. They can bring good luck for the year.
3. the Moon
4. During Tet it is everybody's birthday.
5. the celebrations during Tet
6. someone who is rich or happy so they have good luck that year

Unit 12 – Adventure story worksheet

1. two small, pink flowers
2. a narrow, winding path
3. three tall, pointy towers
4. A young man went on a journey to a faraway land.
5. He saw plenty of amazing scenes.
6. Who designed the wonderful building?
7. small, microscopic
8. thin, lean
9. dreadful, unpleasant
10. Answers will vary.
11. Answers will vary.
12. Answers will vary.

Unit 13 – Factual recount worksheet

1. waits
2. got
3. will ride
4. put
5. brush
6. will take
7. looks; is nodding
8. asked; heard
9. will tell; will notice

Unit 14 – Explanation worksheet

1. habitat, shelter, safe haven
2. explore, search, investigate
3. mature, produce, develop
4. Firstly; then; As a result

Unit 15 – Exposition worksheet

Positive: *wonderful, incredible, confident, certain, support, believe*

Negative: *conflict, annoy, awful, punish, threaten, mistake*